DEVON & CORNWALL

SELECT EDITIONS

Text by Rupert O. Matthews.
Published in Great Britain 1985 by Crown Books.
CLB 1368
Crown Books is a registered imprint of Colour Library Books Ltd.
© 1985 Illustrations and text: Colour Library Books Ltd.,
    Guildford, Surrey, England.
Display and text filmsetting by Acesetters Ltd.,
    Richmond, Surrey, England.
Produced in AGSA, by Barcelona, Spain.
Printed and bound in Barcelona, Spain by Rieusset and Eurobinder.
All rights reserved.
ISBN 0 86283 368 X

The news flashed through Plymouth like wildfire. It was carried through the streets, shouted through the taverns and whispered through the mansions. Drake was back! He only had one ship left of the five which had set sail, but he was back, he was alive and he was incredibly rich. For nearly three years Drake and his Devonmen had been plundering the Spanish Empire in the New World and exactly how much they had stolen nobody is quite sure. Very probably even Francis Drake himself never really knew, but with a ship ballasted with silver, in danger of sinking through the weight of gold and cluttered with chests of diamonds, pearls and emeralds, he was one of the richest men in the world.

On that September day in 1580 Devon leapt from being a rather unregarded English county to being an exciting place known to everyone in Christendom. And although Devon is no longer a haven for adventurous privateers, it is still one of the best-loved of English counties. The beauty of the countryside and the charm of the towns and villages have combined to make it one of the most visited holiday counties in the nation.

Drake's old homeport of Plymouth is one of the largest cities in Devon and has much to offer, despite the devastating bombing of the last war. Indeed, much of the city's modern face sprang from the land cleared by the bombs. The main attraction of the city, however, has always been Plymouth Hoe. It was here that Drake played bowls while awaiting the Spanish Armada and on this commanding height stands a fine statue of the Elizabethan privateer.

A populous conglomeration of quite different character lies to the east around the shores of Tor Bay. Nearly every other house seems to bear the legend 'rooms to let' in the town of Torquay, for this is the Mecca for holidaymakers seeking the bright Cornish sun. Just to the south of the rather grand Torquay is the family resort of Paignton. Though it dates back to Saxon times, Paignton's rise to prosperity began in 1859 when the railway reached the town and made it possible for large numbers of people to come to enjoy the sun and sands.

Away across the lovely countryside north of Tor Bay stands the ancient city of Exeter. Built by the Romans as *Isca Dumnoniorum*, Exeter has survived desertions, sieges and sackings, but no attack was more damaging than that of 1942, when large areas of the city were razed by German bombers. One of the buildings which did survive is the fine cathedral which lies within the city walls. It was originally built after the city surrendered to William the Conqueror in 1068 and incorporated the curious design feature of twin towers flanking the nave. Despite extensive rebuilding in the thirteenth and fourteenth centuries these massive towers remain, their bells pealing out the hours over the rooftops as they have for centuries.

The rich farmland which reaches in a broad swathe from Ilfracombe to Salcombe has long been of the utmost importance to the county. Indeed, long before Devon existed as a county the tribe of the Dumnonii, whose territory covered this area, was one of the most populous and important in Britain. Those wild Celtic tribesmen were skilful farmers, and they were responsible for much of the deforestation of the lowlands and the spread of agricultural and pastoral land. The Romans continued the process and were followed, in turn, by the Anglo-Saxon, medieval and modern farmers, who have completed the process and turned the area from forest into rich, productive arable land. Today, the face of lowland Devon is one of broad fields, swaying grain and well-fed cattle, the epitome of rural peace and prosperity.

How different are the wild landscapes of the moors. Dartmoor covers a vast area of southern Devon and is a land of bare, rolling grassland, muddy morasses and wind-swept tors. As the wind whips across the bleak landscape and squalls of rain drive down the hillsides it is easy to believe the many strange tales that are told of the moor. There is a deep hole at Chaw Gully where a monster guards a fabulous treasure; phantom ponies are heard at Throwleigh; the Wild Hunt gallops the length of the moor and at Postbridge a pair of ghostly hands sometimes grabs steering wheels and drives cars into ditches.

Of all the sights and features of Devon, the one which has become almost mandatory for any visitor to the county, and which has spread beyond its borders, is the Devon tea. A freshly brewed pot of tea accompanied by well baked scones, fruity jam and delicious Devon cream is one of the true pleasures of this delightful county. Sitting in the tea rooms just outside Totnes, sampling just such a delicacy, it is hard to picture Devon as a haunted or violent county. Yet on a velvet-covered table in a tranquil Devon house is a drum, painted with the arms of Sir Francis Drake, which is waiting for the day it shall be played. As the poem has Drake declare:

> Take my drum to England, hang et by the shore,
> Strike et when your powder's runnin' low;
> If the Dons sight Devon, I'll quit the port o' Heaven,
> An' drum them up the Channel as we drumm'd them long ago.

815 King Ecgberht ravaged Cornwall from east to west.

Thus, in one laconic sentence, did a contemporary monk record the demise of Cornwall as a powerful kingdom. That Cornwall did not disappear, as did Brycheiniog and Elmet, is a tribute to the determination and strength of the county which was once a kingdom. It took a century for Cornwall to be incorporated into England as a county, and even then it was too independent and powerful to be granted to just anybody. During the Middle Ages it became traditional to grant the Duchy of Cornwall, with all its attendant lands, soldiers and power, to a member of the Royal Family. Today, the Duke of Cornwall is none other than the Prince of Wales and his estates as Duke combine to make him one of the largest land-owners in the country.

The county itself, however, long ago divorced its fortunes from those of its Duke. The land beyond the Tamar is one of the most beautiful parts of England, combining gentle rural scenes with dramatic windswept heights and a glorious coastline. Far to the west, beyond the tip of Land's End, lie the Isles of Scilly. These are amongst the few possessions of the Duchy of Cornwall to have been handed down from the ancient kingdom. They stand proudly in the gale-lashed Atlantic, growing their flowers in the warm climate which they enjoy. Almost all the wealth of the islands stems from the climate, be it tourism or crops, and the Duchy is trying desperately to diversify an economy based too much on a single commodity.

Beneath the swelling waves, so the stories tell, are the drowned fields, houses and churches of 140 parishes. This was the land of Lyonnesse, once ridden by King Arthur and his noble knights, and even today the spires, towers and walls of the sunken land can be glimpsed beneath the waves. Apart from the Scillies, the only part of Lyonesse to remain is the rock that is St Michael's Mount. At low tide the Mount is linked to the mainland by a broad causeway of sand, but at high tide the sea comes racing in across the sands and glittering, blue sea separates the two.

Tales of King Arthur surface again far to the northeast, on the north coast at Tintagel. It is said that he was born here and spirited away by the magician Merlin to be brought up in safety far from his father's domains. Whether or not the stories are true, there are the remains of an ancient monastery on the site, which was built in Arthurian times, and the sheer beauty of the location makes any tale believable. This is the north coast of Cornwall at its best. Towering cliffs rise to dizzying heights above the crashing surf which has rolled in from the Atlantic, and seabirds wheel in the sky. Long lines of jagged rocks reach out into the spray-spattered sea as the ancient, hard rocks of Cornwall resist the force of the ocean.

Such a coast seems a thousand miles from the gentle sands of Newquay. The town gets its name from the four-hundred-year-old quay which was built to serve the increasingly numerous fishermen of Towan Blystra. Both coasts are echoed to the south, where sandy bays and superb harbours alternate with steep headlands. It is along this coast that the main towns and cities are strung.

Penzance lies tucked in the bay behind Land's End and was the first of the Cornish towns to become a resort during Victorian days. Before then it had existed in quiet prosperity based upon tin mining and smuggling; that most Cornish of crimes. The story went around town that headless horses pulled a doomed coach through the streets and, whether true or not, the tale was used as a cover by the smugglers, among whom the mayor was prominent. Today, the miles of beach pull the holiday makers, just as they do at Falmouth, some miles to the east. Here there is also a thriving port and industrial area, carefully hidden to the north of the beaches and tourist attractions. The third of the coastal towns of Cornwall is St Austell, a town built on clay, both literally and economically.

Over the hills north of St Austell lies the county town of Bodmin. It was this town which throughout the Mediaeval and Tudor years found reason after reason to rebel against the Crown and their Duke. Whether it was taxes, a pretender to the throne or religion, almost any local issue was good enough for the men of Bodmin to take arms and march east. Truro, by contrast, remained quiescent and steadily grew in size and prosperity, aquiring city status and fine architecture.

But Bodmin has a claim to fame which is unique in the county. It has given its name to one of the wildest and most romantic stretches of land in Cornwall: Bodmin Moor. For miles the wind-blasted heath stretches away to the horizon, broken only by a lonely car on a lonely road. High on the moor, far from human habitation, is a lake a mile in circumference which is not fed by any stream, nor by any other visible means. Dozmary Pool is its name and legends tell how, after the fateful battle of Camlann, Sir Bedivere came here at King Arthur's request and flung Excalibur far out into the lake. Cornwall may have been an English county for a thousand years, but it has kept its unique legends and its identity throughout.

Above: Clovelly, on the north Devon coast.

Facing page: Chapel of Our Lady, Exeter Cathedral. Above: Clovelly.

Above: Salcombe, with its wooded hills and sandy bays, is one of the most beautifully sited towns in England. Top: a canal near Tiverton. Right: the River Exe flows past a pub at Bickleigh. Overleaf left: Torquay. Overleaf right: Torgross and Slapton Sands, which separate the fresh-water lake of Slapton Ley from the sea.

Left and above left: the cobbled streets of Clovelly, one of the great tourist showplaces of the county. Above right: a thatched cottage at Bucks Mills. Top: the granite church of St Pancras at Widecombe-in-the-Moor raises its 135-foot, 16th-century tower above the wild landscape of Dartmoor. Overleaf: Cockington Forge, Torquay.

The carved woodwork of Devon's churches is amongst the best in the country and includes the gilded screen at Plymtree (top) and the lectern (above left) and bench ends (above right) at Ashprington. Right: the 15th-century church at Combe Martin. Overleaf: two aerial views of Plymouth, Drake's home town, with (left) the Royal Citadel, a 17th-century fortress, and the green sward of the Hoe.

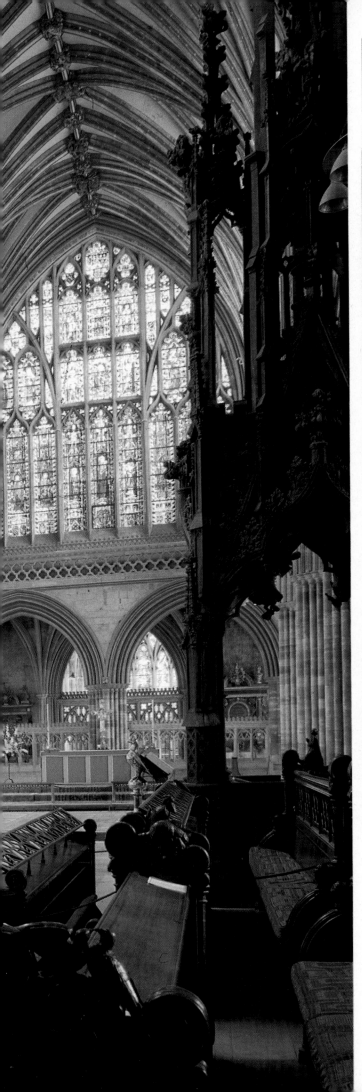

Left: the choir and chancel of Exeter Cathedral. The see came to Exeter in 1050, but the choir and chancel date only from the late thirteenth century, when the magnificent Decorated Gothic style was in fashion. The fine ribbed vaulting is unique in that it runs 300 uninterrupted feet for the entire length of the cathedral, the twin Norman towers being positioned on either side of the nave. Above: the interior of the church at Braunton, an ancient church renowned for its carved benchends. Top: Lapford Church. The picturesque fishing port of Brixham (overleaf), on Tor Bay, was the first landing place in England for William of Orange when he came to claim the throne in 1688 as William III.

Left: Torquay is the largest and best served resort in Devon. Top: the spectacular red cliffs and gentle farmland which surround Sidmouth. Above left: the elegant fan vaulting of 1526 to be found in the Lane Aisle of Cullompton Church. Above right: the pulpit of Ashprington Church. Overleaf left: Harcombe. Overleaf right: Mothecombe Bay.

Four centuries ago, when ships were smaller than they are today, Ilfracombe (left) was an important port. After the close of the Tudor period the town turned to fishing for its livelihood and more recently tourism has taken over, making it the largest resort on the north coast. Brentor (top) must be one of the most isolated churches in the county, perched on its 1,100-foot-high hill. The church is encircled by earthwork defences which date back hundreds of years to the days of the warring Celtic tribes that preceded the Romans. Above left: the small village of Clovelly, which has remained almost unchanged, apart from the hordes of tourists, since it was 'discovered' by Dickens last century. Overleaf: the wild crags of the Valley of the Rocks, near Lynton, which inspired Shelley.

Clovelly (these pages) is unique amongst English villages in that it is closed to motor traffic, a car park being provided on the outskirts. Exeter gained its bishopric in 1050 when Bishop Leofric abandoned Crediton for the better-defended Exeter. After 1107 the Normans built the two transpetal towers (overleaf right), while the harmonious vaulting (overleaf left) was completed years later by Richard Farleigh, the architect of Salisbury's fine steeple.

When William the Conqueror finally captured Exeter two years after the Battle of Hastings, he thereby imposed his authority on Devon. One of the most solid signs of the changing times came when the Saxon cathedral was demolished and a Norman edifice built in its place. In turn, most of the Norman church has been replaced by the splendid Gothic cathedral we see today (left). Overleaf: houses in the Cathedral grounds. Top: the charming church of St Peter at Cornworthy. Basically of 14th century construction, this church has a fine Georgian interior. The granite church of Bridford lies near Dartmoor and boasts a splendid rood screen (above) made in 1508.

Above and top: Widecombe-in-the-Moor, the Dartmoor scene of the fair to which Old Uncle Tom Cobleigh and his companions went in the famous song. Right: Kingswear, on the Dart Estuary, provides a rail terminus for Dartmouth. Overleaf left: shops in the centre of Exeter. Tiverton (overleaf right) was one of the first English towns in Devon and is today a thriving agricultural and industrial town.

Top: the Dartmoor village of Buckland-in-the-Moor, on the banks of the Dart, the combination of stone and thatch is typical of moor villages. Above left: Clovelly. Above right: Bowerman's Nose on Dartmoor, the great, windswept upland of the county. The moor was once fairly heavily inhabited, but a combination of declining mines, agricultural slump and the Black Death emptied it in the fourteenth century. Right: the mile-long beach at Seaton, near the mouth of the Yarty. Overleaf: Jacob's Ladder at Sidmouth.

Teignmouth (left) is one of the oldest Cornish resorts. Above: the River Exe at Bickleigh. Top: St Andrew's Church at Cullompton, built in 1430. Overleaf: two aerial views of Dartmouth, dominated by the Naval College.

On the highest hill in Dartmouth stands the Royal Naval College (below), which was completed in 1905 to the plans of Sir Aston Webb. Riding at moorings in the harbour at Brixham is a full scale replica of the *Golden Hind* (right). It was in this ship, then called the *Pelican*, that Francis Drake set sail in 1577 to harass the Spanish Empire. The four ships which accompanied the *Golden Hind* suffered various fates, ranging from shipwreck to getting lost, and only Drake's ship reached the Pacific safely. He then proceeded to plunder towns and ships with impunity, taking gold,

silver and jewels beyond number before continuing across the Pacific to pick up valuable spices from the Moluccas. Upon his return to Devon waters in 1580 Drake's first concern was whether Queen Elizabeth was still on the throne, for any other monarch may have had him executed. Elizabeth was alive, however, and knighted Drake on board the *Golden Hind*. In the hills behind the town are several caves which were inhabited during the Stone Age and have yielded many bones and remains of interest to scientists. Overleaf: Lester Point at Combe Martin, a village which was once known for its silver mines but is now associated with the glorious coastline hereabouts.

Top: Combe Martin, as its name might suggest, lies in a combe reaching down to the sea. The rather untidy straggle of houses which tumbles down the slopes has no plan, but reveals a peculiar charm which is unique to this village. The entrances to the mediaeval silver mines can still be traced, though it is no longer possible to follow them under the main street. The small beach is both pebble and sand, the incoming sea covering the broad reach of sand which is so popular at low tide. Above: Hoops Inn. Right: the beach seen from Orcombe Point, Exmouth. This town has long been famed for its bathing beaches, having attracted people from Exeter as far back as the early 18th century. Sheepstor (overleaf left) is one of the more appealing Dartmoor villages, lying on the southwestern slopes of the plateau. The churchyard contains the tomb of Sir James Brooke, the English merchant who, in the 1840s, made himself Rajah of Sarawak and initiated the family rule which was to last a hundred years. Overleaf right: the nearby Burrator Woods.

Top: Ilfracombe, the Victorian holiday resort on Devon's north coast. During the long Napoleonic Wars fashionable society was unable to travel abroad and Ilfracombe was one of several Devon towns to benefit from a growth in the holiday trade. The town's charm and popularity have not diminished since, and its small harbour is a constant delight. Dartington Hall (above) is one the finest secular mediaeval buildings in the entire southwest. It was built in the closing years of the fourteenth century by John Holland, half-brother to King Richard II, on an estate at least six centuries older still. It is, today, one of the most progressive educational and research establishments in the country, with a college of art, a school and thousands of acres of land. Right: the quayside at Brixham, showing the replica Tudor warship and the monument to William III. Overleaf: Exmouth.

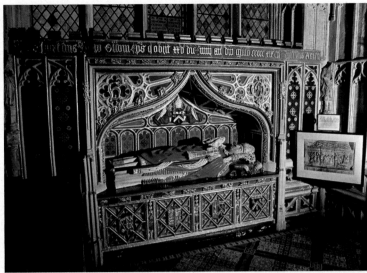

Exeter Cathedral (left) contains many fine examples of
ecclesiastical architecture from various periods. The tomb
of Bishop Oldham (top) stands in a chantry chapel off the
south choir aisle dedicated to St Saviour and St Boniface.
Sir Walter Raleigh was born in the house (above), in Hayes
Barton, in 1554. This son of a Devon knight went on to hold
some of the highest appointments in the land under Elizabeth
I, only to be sent to the block by her successor, James I.
Overleaf left: a commemoratory plaque in the Barbican area
of Plymouth. Overleaf right, top: an aerial view of
Dartmouth. Overleaf right, bottom: the clifftop village of
Bigbury-on-Sea.

PILGRIM FATHERS WHO SAILED FROM HERE
THE BARBICAN, PLYMOUTH, IN THE MAYFLOWER, 1620

MASTER WILL BRADFORD	- FUSTIAN MAKER AUSTERF'D, YORKS
JOHN CARVER	- MERCHANT OF DONCASTER.
MASTER EDW'D WINSLOW	- PRINTER OF DROITWICH.
MASTER WILL BREWSTER	- POSTMASTER, TUTOR, ETC.
MASTER ISAAC ALLERTON	- TAILOR OF LONDON.
CAPT. MYLES STANDISH	- SOLDIER OF CHORLEY, LANCS.
MASTER STEP'N HOPKINS	- WOTTON UNDER EDGE GLOUCS'TR.
MASTER CHRIS MARTIN	- GREAT BURSTEAD ESSEX.
MASTER WILL MULLINS	- SHOPKEEPER DORKING, SURREY.
MASTER WILL WHITE	- WOOL CARDER.
MASTER RICH WARREN	- MERCHANT OF LONDON.
EDWARD TILLEY	- CLOTH MAKER OF LONDON.
JOHN TILLEY	- SILK WORKER OF LONDON.
PETER BROWNE	- GREAT BURSTEAD ESSEX.
FRANCIS EATON	- CARPENTER OF BRISTOL.
FRANCIS COOK	- WOOL COMBER OF BLYTH.
THOMAS ENGLISH	- MARINER.
THOMAS TINKER	- WOOD SAWYER.
THOMAS ROGERS	- MERCHANT.
JOHN RINGDALE	- LONDON.
EDWARD FULLER	- REDENHALL NORFOLK.
JOHN TURNER	- MERCHANT.
JAMES CHILTON	- TAILOR OF CANTERBURY.
JOHN CRACKSTON	- COLCHESTER.
JOHN BILLINGTON	- LONDON.
RICH BRITTERIDGE	- GREAT BURSTEAD ESSEX.
RICHARD GARDINER	- HARWICH ESSEX.
MOSES FLETCHER	- SMITH OF SANDWICH.
JOHN ALDEN	- COOPER OF HARWICH.
SAMUEL FULLER	- SAIL MAKER.
JOHN GOODMAN	- LINEN WEAVER.
DEGORY PRIEST	- HATTER OF LONDON.
THOMAS WILLIAMS	- YARMOUTH NORFOLK.
JOHN ALLERTON	- MARINER.
JOHN HOOKE	- SERVANT BOY.
RICHARD MORE	- LONDON.
ROGER WILDER	- MAN SERVANT.
WILLIAM LATHAM	- SERVANT BOY.
JOHN HOWLAND	- LONDON.
WILLIAM BUTTEN	- AUSTEREIELD.
RICHARD CLARKE	- EDMOND MARGESON.
GILBERT WINSLOW	- JASPER MORE.
EDWARD DOTEY	- EDWARD LEISTER.
JOHN LANGEMORE	- ROBERT CARTER.
WILLIAM HOLBECK	- EDWARD THOMPSON.
GEORGE SOULE	- ELIAS STORY.

Knight Hayes.

Gwithian's Lighthouse stands on the horizon, beyond Gwithian Sands.

St Ives is one of the most picturesque of the Cornish resorts, having retained many of its older buildings around the harbour (these pages).

Perhaps the most secure natural harbour for small craft on the north Cornwall Coast is Boscastle (left). The narrow, winding entrance and towering cliffs provide almost perfect protection from the ocean waves, whichever direction they are running. In the shelter of this inlet a thriving fishing and sealing port grew up, until the lack of a rail link caused a decline. Land's End, by contrast, is wide open to all that the wild Atlantic can throw at it. The pounding breakers sweep in from the west to spend their fury on the jagged cliffs and rocks around the headland (below, bottom and overleaf). Marking the hazard to shipping is the Longships Lighthouse (below).

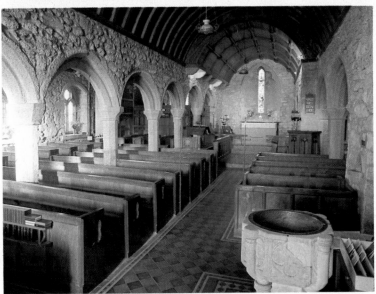

Perhaps no structures in Cornwall are as evocative as
its churches, for after the Roman evacuation of Britain
in the fifth century, Cornwall was one of the few
regions to keep Christianity alive throughout the pagan
onslaught. Left: the lonely hilltop church of St
Endellion, with its fine wagon-roof. Above: the 12th-
century nave of Zennor Church. Top: the intricate 19th-
century rood screen of Blisland Church. Overleaf, left:
romantic St Michael's Mount at high tide. Overleaf,
right: Coverack, with its lifeboat station.

One day in 1864, 75 million pilchards are said to have been
landed at the small town of St Ives (overleaf), whose
fishing industry has now been replaced by tourism. Fishing
of another kind is still carried on at East Looe (top),
which is the main British centre for shark-fishing. The
picturesque qualities of this port, where smuggling was
once rife, have made it one of the most crowded of Cornish
villages in the summer months. Above: the curious formation
of Bedruthan's Steps, north of Newquay. Left: the Treen
Cliffs, near Land's End.

Falmouth Harbour (top) is by far the busiest in the county, being able to cope with ships of up to 100,000 tons. The resort of Falmouth presents a different face, with the mildest climate in Britain and numerous facilities. Far smaller, but perhaps more attractive, are the village ports of Cadgwith (above), Polperro (left and overleaf, left) and Mevagissey (overleaf, right).

St Michael's Mount (right) features strongly in Arthurian Cornish legend, for it is said that this is all that remains of the lost land of Lyonnesse. It was from here that Tristram left to bring Iseult as a bride to King Mark of Cornwall only to fall in love with her himself, thus providing inspiration for one of Cornwall's greatest romances. In 1044 King Edward the Confessor gave St Michael's Mount to a Norman monastic order and a monastery was founded on the island. In 1425 the Mount was taken back by the Crown and the present castle constructed on this highly defensible site. At high tide the Mount becomes an island as the sea floods the sands and the cobbled causeway which usually link it with the mainland. Newquay (above) takes its name from a quay built in the 16th century for the fishing town of Towan Blystra. Top: the small harbour at Mevagissey. Overleaf: boats beached at Cadgwith.

St Mawes (right) takes its name from the Celtic monk who for many years lived as a hermit beside the well. Today the well, whose waters were once renowned as a cure for worms, stands near the Victory Inn. The town stands across the Carrick Roads from Falmouth and presents a more gracious air than its neighbour. Below: Polperro. Bottom: boats moored in the harbour at St Ives. Overleaf left: the rocky headland of Land's End. Overleaf right: Bude, a town whose wave-pounded shores were once notorious for shipwrecks, and have now made it popular as a surfing venue.

Polperro (left) lies in a steep-sided valley on Cornwall's south coast and is one of the most unspoilt fishing villages in the county despite the hordes of visitors which descend on it every summer. The tiny harbour is lined with houses rising sheer from the water and dotted with various small craft. Zennor (top) huddles around its church dedicated to St Senara, from whom the village name is derived. The church is the centre of a romantic legend. Many years ago, says the story, a mermaid was attracted by the beautiful singing of Matthew Trewalla, the squire's son, and used all her wiles to lure Trewalla to her home beneath the waves, where his singing can still be heard. A carved pew-end commemorates the story. Above: two of the fine, late-Mediaeval stained glass windows from St Neot's beautiful church. The Scilly Isles, (overleaf) St Mary's, stand some 28 miles off Land's End, though the ferry service runs over a distance of 40 miles from Penzance. Only five of the 140 islands are populated, a testimony to their ruggedness and small size.

Right: Whitesand Bay, which lies just to the north of
Land's End. Below: the cold light of dawn lightens the sky
over St Michael's Mount as high tide covers the sands of
the bay. Visits to the battlemented castle and 14th-century
church which crown the rock must be carefully timed as only
boats can make the crossing at high tide. Overleaf: two
distinct aerial views of Newquay, the most popular seaside
resort in the county. Its immense popularity rests on the
fine surf-fringed beaches rather than its town, for there
are far prettier ports and villages along the nearby coast.

Of the flourishing fishing port which existed in Newquay
before the railway came in 1875, the Huer's House is a rare
survivor. It was in this cliff-top house that the huer
watched for the coming of the pilchards. In days gone by
the shoals of pilchards were so vast that when they entered
the bay the sea turned red. The railway was built as part
of a scheme to export china clay through the port, but the
harbour was not large enough for the increasingly busy
trade. Eventually, the railway came to carry far more
passengers than freight as the quality of the sands brought
holiday-makers to Newquay in droves.

Left: Newquay Harbour, which is today on the edge of the town. Penzance harbour (above) provides shelter for one the lightships which lie anchored off the coast to warn shipping of shallows and treacherous waters. The town was the victim of the smouldering warfare with Spain which rumbled on for many years after the defeat of the Armada in 1588. In 1595, 600 Spaniards landed to burn and pillage the town, which they did successfully until a local force led by Sir Francis Godolphin drove them off. It suffered again during the Civil War, but thereafter gained prominence as one of the county's stannary towns to which all mined tin had to be brought for assaying and taxation. The concentration of mining in the area led to science and technology being favoured local pastimes, culminating in Humphry Davy's invention of the miner's safety lamp in 1815. Overleaf: the cliffs near Land's End.

Scattered across the face of Cornwall are several castles
and strongholds, of which the ruins of Launceston (below
left) are an outstanding example. It is of the Norman
'motte and bailey' type of construction, but is unusual in
that it was built of stone and has survived almost
unchanged – the tall, artificial mound of the motte being
clearly crowned by its stone defensive tower. Far more
imposing and romantic are the shattered walls of Tintagel
(right). The ruins that stand on this dramatic spit of land
are the remnants of a castle built in 1145 for Reginald,
illegitimate son of Henry I, and the then Earl of Cornwall.
It was abandoned during the fifteenth century and has been
left to decline ever since. For many years the site has
been associated with King Arthur, though only a monastery
on the peninsula dates from Arthurian times. Below right:
the harbour at St Ives. Bottom: Longships Lighthouse off
Land's End. Overleaf: Towan Head, near Torquay.

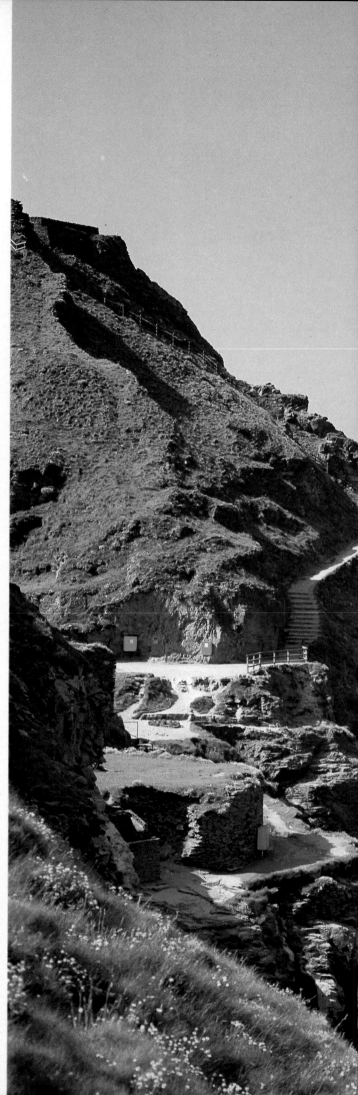

The dramatic, towering rocks of the beach at Perranporth (top) provide some of the most spectacular bathing scenery in Cornwall. Of more importance to the village are the lovely sands which blanket the shore. Eight centuries ago the shifting sands moved inland and inundated the 7th-century parish church. The inhabitants then built another church on higher ground to the east. But once again the sand marched irresistibly on, and in the fifteenth century the new church had to be abandoned, its site marked only by a stone cross. The most recent church is that at Perranzabuloe, a corruption of the name St Piran in Sabulo (St Piran in the sand). In 1835 the story had an interesting sequel when the original church was rediscovered and dug out of the embracing sand. It is now guarded from the dunes by a surrounding concrete shell. Left and overleaf, left: the fine beach and houses of St Ives. Above: the broken rocks and sheer faces of Treen Cliffs. Overleaf right: the small village of Cadgwith.

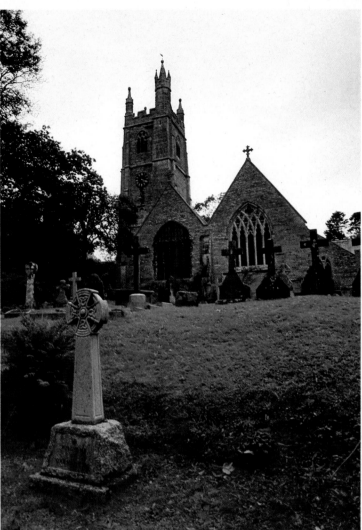

Mullion Cove (left) has a cave which can only be reached at low tide. Top: St Mawgan in Pydar, which dates back to the 13th century. Above: Cape Cornwall, near St Just. Overleaf left: Penzance Harbour. Overleaf right: Porth Navas.

Top: the Longships Lighthouse from the air. Above left: a fisherman displays his catch in Cadgwith. Above right: Polperro. Right: the rugged, fractured cliffs around Land's End. Mousehole (overleaf) has had more than its fair share of bad luck over the years. It was the first village to be pillaged by the Spaniards in 1595 and, more recently, lost many of its men in a lifeboat disaster at sea.

When the tide runs out many of the drowned river valleys, or rias, of Cornwall are exposed as broad mudflats cut by a small stream. The Looe Estuary (right) is lined by grassy fields and tree-covered hills and sports boats stranded on the mudflats. The town of Looe was, until 1883, the two towns of East and West Looe. Though today the town is small and tranquil, the original two were once of vital importance to the nation. East Looe contributed 20 ships and 315 men to the Royal expedition to Calais in 1346, only 5 less ships than London. Thereafter, the two towns slipped

into relative obscurity with a prosperity based upon the typical Cornish industries of fishing and smuggling. Above: in the warm rays of the setting sun, surf pounds the rocks along Cape Cornwall, just north of Land's End. Overleaf left: Talland Bay, which takes its name from the saint to whom the local parish church is dedicated: St Tallanus. Overleaf right: Mousehole, clustered around its crescent-shaped port. It was here that Dolly Pentreath, the last known native speaker of Cornish, died in 1777.

Mevagissey (left) is a bustling village where small shops and brightly painted fishing craft crowd the harbour below the cottages. Above: Polperro. Top: St Michael's Mount at low tide, when the stone causeway stands revealed above the water. The South West Peninsula Coastal Path is one of the most dramatic walks in England, encompassing such scenery as Land's End (overleaf left) and Pentire Head (overleaf right).

Above: the surf-fringed headland of Cape Cornwall.